RESTORING those WHO FALL
A Church Discipline Statement

Jim Elliff & Daryl Wingerd

www.CCWtoday.org

Copyright © 2006 Christ Fellowship of Kansas City
Revised 2008

ISBN 978-0-9745253-9-6

Scripture taken from The Holy Bible, New King James Version
Copyright 1982, 1991 by Thomas Nelson, Inc.

Additional copies of *Restoring Those Who Fall* and other
publications may be ordered online at www.CCWtoday.org.

Published by Christian Communicators Worldwide
Kansas City (Parkville), Missouri, USA

Cover design by Tony Barmann

www.CCWtoday.org

Contents

Foreword 4

Introduction 5

1. Minor Faults 6

2. Unverifiable Sins 6

3. Personal Offenses 7

4. Public Disobedience 8

5. Insufferable Wickedness 11

Additional Considerations 13

Scripture Passages Related to Church Discipline 18

Foreword

The Head of the church has instructed us to practice church discipline. Since believers have no option but to obey, it is customary for serious-minded churches to compile the relevant Scripture passages and formulate a comprehensive plan of action. This prepares them to act lovingly and swiftly when a member perpetuates his disobedience or commits a serious offense. *Restoring Those Who Fall* is a policy statement designed to be adopted by churches that consider it a faithful representation of Christ's instructions.*

Christian fellowship is too precious to forfeit through disobedience or sinful neglect. Yet, if we fail to become accountable to each other and to the Lord, we are risking even more than this—we also lose a more potent witness in the community. Above all, the individual who is sinning and unrepentant is not being loved properly when the church fails to act. It is uncaring not to seek his restoration in a biblical manner, and it is unloving not to remove him from fellowship if he shows the marks of being unregenerate. Failure to expel him may prolong his deception, while removal from membership may eventually open his eyes to see his true condition before Christ.

If we were not commanded to correct those who disobey, we could afford to delay adopting a discipline policy, but we do not have this option. We hope this statement helps curb sin and brings many back from disobedience.

Jim Elliff and Daryl Wingerd

---

*If adaptations are made to this booklet, we suggest that they be inserted in the booklet, or pasted inside the back cover.

Restoring Those Who Fall
A Church Discipline Statement

Church discipline is one of the primary means God uses to correct and restore His children when they fall into sin. It is also one way in which He maintains the unity, purity, integrity, and reputation of the church. Through private or public instruction, warning, counsel, or rebuke, and even social avoidance or expulsion from membership, God corrects his disobedient children or removes those who are not truly His. Christ Himself declared the church to be heaven's instrument in carrying out this difficult but necessary function (Matthew 18:15-20).

The purpose of this statement is to define, in general terms, five classes of sinful behavior for which church discipline may be necessary,* and to explain how the Bible tells us to respond to each. We must not assume, however, that every situation will fall neatly into a single category. Disciplinary matters are often confusing combinations or variations of these general classes, making the proper course of action difficult to determine. For this reason, the church must carry out discipline with prayer, diligent application of Scripture, and reliance upon the Spirit of God.

---

*The authors are indebted to Rev. Eleazer Savage who published *A Manual of Church Discipline* in 1845. It is difficult to find a complete copy of this work, but a helpful portion is published in the book, *Polity: Biblical Arguments on How to Conduct Church Life*, edited by Mark Dever, (Washington D.C.: Center for Church Reform, 2001.), pp. 479-523.

1. Minor Faults

Minor faults are attitudes and actions such as rudeness, impatience, grumbling, complaining, negativity, pettiness, boasting, irritability, speaking too much or when inappropriate, lack of trust, worry, timidity, and selfishness. We are permitted, and actually encouraged, to overlook most minor faults rather than resorting to discipline (Proverbs 10:12; 19:11; 1 Peter 4:8).

If a minor fault seems serious enough to require private counsel, we should be particularly careful to apply Christ's words about removing the "speck" from our brother's eye while a "plank" is in our own (Matthew 7:1-5). Only if a minor fault is repeated so consistently or in such a disruptive manner that it causes harm to the church will any measure(s) be taken beyond private instruction, warning, and/or rebuke.

2. Unverifiable Sins

Whether minor or serious, unverifiable sins are offenses that are known to only one church member in addition to the offender(s). Additionally, no concrete evidence could be brought forth as proof. Unverifiable sins might include insulting words spoken in private, physical assault or theft where no physical or circumstantial evidence exists, breach of a private verbal contract, and private awareness of another member's illicit behavior.

In such cases, it may be necessary for the offended person or lone witness to rebuke the offender privately. If private rebuke is unsuccessful and the offender is not willing to admit his sin to others, normally no further action may be taken. The matter must be left with God; it should not be revealed to anyone else (Deuteronomy 19:15; Proverbs 25:8-10). It must also be recognized that the one being accused of an unverifiable sin may, in fact, be innocent or misunderstood.

Exceptions to this rule concerning silence include the reporting of criminal offenses to the proper authorities when necessary or required by law. Also, if the unverifiable sinful action is of such a nature that it likely would affect a person's involvement in the church, or poses a danger to others, the member should speak to an elder about it. The elder may have received other information about this individual that would verify the action(s) in question (such as a past history known only to the elder, or a similar report from another church member). If this is the case, additional action will be necessary. In all situations involving unverifiable sins, the individual in question is innocent until proven guilty.

3. Personal Offenses

Personal offenses are those that occur between two Christians—more specifically, two members of the same church. Personal offenses could be defined as any sinful behavior by one member that causes harm to another. A representative list of these sins would include insults, slander, breach of personal trust or contract, physical or sexual abuse, adultery, physical assault, theft, and vandalism.

In these situations, the offended person must closely follow Matthew 18:15-17. He must first meet with the offender in private, explain his offense to him, and seek his repentance (Matthew 18:15).

If the offender remains unrepentant, the offended person must be cautious before taking additional measures. If the offense is unverifiable (as defined above) or not serious enough to warrant bringing to the attention of other church members, it should not be pursued further. If the offense is significant and verifiable, a meeting will be arranged, during which the offended person may present his case to the offender in the presence of one or two other members (Matthew 18:16). These should either be witnesses to the offense or mature, discerning members who are able to evaluate evidence and testimony, question both parties effectively, determine guilt or responsibility, and offer appropriate biblical counsel.

If the offender remains unrepentant even after his guilt has been proven before witnesses, the matter will be told to the general membership of the church at another meeting (Matthew 18:17). If the offender is present, the elder(s) will rebuke him publicly and implore him to confess and repent. If he is absent, the matter will still be revealed to the church (in appropriately limited detail). In either case, the members of the church will be encouraged to make personal efforts to persuade him to repent. A date will be set for a final meeting where the matter will be brought to conclusion. The offender will be notified regarding this meeting (in a verifiable way, such as certified mail) and encouraged to attend in the hope that he will make a public confession. Because the offender's guilt has already been established, no opportunity will be given at these subsequent meetings for him to debate the matter or defend himself publicly.

At the final meeting, the offender (if present) will be offered another opportunity to repent and be restored. If he remains unrepentant or is not present, he will be considered an unbeliever and expelled from membership (Matthew 18:17). Even if the offender repents, restitution and/or other remedial actions may be necessary as determined by the elders (e.g., mandated accountability, removal from church office, and/or counseling).

4. Public Disobedience

Public disobedience is sinful behavior that causes harm to the unity, doctrinal integrity, purity, or reputation of the church as a whole. This category would include, for example, false teaching, divisiveness, contentions, gossip, slander of the church or its leaders, insubordination, sexual immorality, drunkenness, covetousness, theft, dishonesty, outbursts of anger or fighting, foul language, willful failure to provide, wrongful divorce or remarriage, and breach of public trust or contract.

Unlike the precise instructions for resolving personal offenses (Matthew 18:15-17), the instructions for dealing with acts of public disobedience are varied. Especially here, we must pause, pray, seek wise counsel, and apply the Scriptures carefully, considering each situation to be unique.

The following are the procedures found in the New Testament for handling public disobedience. Not all measures listed here will be appropriate for each situation. We have listed them in order of severity, from the most gentle or subtle to the most direct, but this should not be construed to mean that they will be applied in this order. It may sometimes be necessary to bypass these measures altogether and proceed directly to expulsion from membership (see section 5, "Insufferable Wickedness").

- **Be watchful** (Acts 20:28-31; Hebrews 12:14-16). We should not aggressively hunt for offenses or opportunities to enact discipline (Matthew 13:28-30), but we must be vigilant and ready to address sinful behavior when it becomes known. This is particularly the responsibility of the elders who are the shepherds of the flock. The New Testament warns that there will be some who profess to be Christians who will seek to harm the church (Acts 20:30; 2 Peter 2:1-3). A person who practices and/or promotes sinful behavior, teaches contrary to sound doctrine, is divisive or insubordinate, or exalts himself (3 John 9-10) may be a "wolf in sheep's clothing."

- **Correct through teaching** (2 Timothy 2:24-26; Titus 1:9). The Word of God is powerful and effective. In all cases, especially when more direct or severe measures are not immediately necessary, elders and other teachers will address disobedience by applying the Scriptures humbly, gently, patiently, and convincingly (also see 2 Timothy 3:16-4:2).

- **Plead with the offender(s)** (1 Corinthians 1:10-11; Philippians 4:2-3). Paul pleaded with the Corinthian church as a group, and with Euodia and Syntyche as individual Christians in Philippi, imploring them to stop being divisive or contentious. In both situations, his pleas, which were in open letters to the churches, also served as gentle public rebukes.

- **Warn them of consequences** (1 Thessalonians 5:14; 2 Thessalonians 3:14-15; Titus 3:10-11). Unruly or disobedient Christians who have not responded to gentle or subtle disciplinary measures are exposing themselves to public rebuke, social avoidance, or even expulsion from the church. When appropriate, we will warn them of these embarrassing and painful consequences. Most importantly, we will tell them of the day when they will stand before the Lord Jesus to be judged according to their deeds (2 Corinthians 5:9-11).

- **Rebuke them** (Galatians 2:11-14; 1 Timothy 5:19-20; Titus 1:13; 2:15). The prospect of being rebuked, either publicly or privately, should be a powerful deterrent to sinful behavior. Public rebuke also serves the purpose of teaching by identifying and exposing the nature of error (Ephesians 5:8-13). When carried out in the presence of the church, this type of corrective action is a pastoral responsibility. It should never happen without prior planning and agreement among the church's leadership.

- **Silence them** (Titus 1:9-11). Paul insisted that false teachers and divisive people "must be silenced," and his implication was that the *leaders* of the church should make every effort to silence them. There might be a variety of levels at which this can be applied. For example, the elders may forbid them to speak at meetings, instruct them not to discuss certain matters with other church members, or remove them from teaching positions.

- **Shame them through social avoidance** (2 Thessalonians 3:6-15). This rare church action becomes appropriate when a church member begins to lead an idle or disorderly life that falls short of gross immorality, but nevertheless disturbs the church. The other members of the church should demonstrate that such behavior is unacceptable in their midst by temporarily (meaning as long as necessary) excluding the unruly brother or sister from all fellowship. Such a person, for example, would not be welcome at church gatherings or in members' homes as a dinner guest until his or her ungodly and/or disorderly behavior ended. In appearance, the church's treatment of such a person would be similar to the exclusion commanded in 1 Corinthians 5 and Matthew 18:17. The difference is that the person would still be considered a Christian and a member of the church. If this shunning action does not produce repentance within a reasonable (relatively brief) period of time, the offense will be considered "insufferable wickedness" (see section 5). (Note: The reference in Romans 16:17 to avoiding certain people almost certainly refers to outsiders, not members of the church.)

5. Insufferable Wickedness

Insufferable wickedness refers to situations where there is only one proper course of action—expulsion from membership. The difference between the same types of sins mentioned under "public disobedience" (section 4) and "insufferable wickedness" (section 5), is, generally speaking, a matter of degree rather than type. A member who begins to form a habit of getting drunk, for example, will most likely be dealt with in one or more of the ways described under "public disobedience," while one who has become publicly known as a "drunkard" will be expelled immediately. In some instances, however, the type of sin, even if committed only once, may warrant immediate expulsion.

There are three kinds of offenders whose behavior will be considered insufferable and who will therefore be expelled:

- **Unrepentant Offenders**
  These are church members who have refused to acknowledge their sin and repent, even after public rebuke and exhortation from the entire church (Matthew 18:17).

- **Gross Offenders**
  These are members who commit even a single sin that is so abhorrent, shameful, or notorious that the reputation of Christ and the church is imperiled if they are not immediately expelled (1 Corinthians 5).

- **Offenders Who Are Known by Their Wickedness**
  These are members who have become known publicly for sins like heresy, apostasy, divisiveness, sexual immorality, drunkenness, or covetousness.* Their sinful lifestyle makes them indistinguishable from unbelievers. In others words, they are so characterized by false beliefs, false teaching, destructive motives, worldly affections, or immoral living that they cannot, by definition, be considered Christians (1 Corinthians 5:11-13; 6:9-10; Galatians 5:19-21; Titus 1:16; 1 John 1:5-6; 2:3-4; 3:9-10; 2 John 9-11).

In these situations, all that is necessary before expulsion is the establishment of the facts. We must notice that in 1 Corinthians 5, Paul did not instruct the church to first warn the incestuous man or seek his repentance. No command was given to rebuke him, publicly or privately, before expelling him. With the man's gross immorality well-known to all, Paul told them to immediately expel him from the church (1 Corinthians 5:5, 13).

---

*In our wealthy and materialistic society, Christians often tend to trivialize covetousness, but Paul calls it idolatry, and lists it as one of a number of sins that are bringing the wrath of God "upon the sons of disobedience" (Colossians 3:5-6). Concerning the love (or coveting) of money, Paul told Timothy that it was "a root of all kinds of evil" (1 Timothy 6:10). John was speaking of covetousness when he wrote, "Do not love the world or the things in the world. If anyone loves the world, the love of the Father is not in him" (1 John 2:15). "Do not be deceived," Paul wrote to the church at Corinth. No covetous person "will inherit the kingdom of God" (1 Corinthians 6:9-10).

In verse 11 of the same chapter, Paul lists other types of offenders who must be treated in the same way.

Even if sorrow and repentance are initially expressed by one who commits insufferable wickedness, expulsion from the church is still necessary in order to maintain the reputation of Christ and His church. Though the offender's repentance may be genuine, a time of proving is required before this can be known for sure, and before membership privileges can be restored. Persons expelled by church discipline, if truly repentant, may come back into fellowship through the normal procedure for church membership.

Additional Considerations:

1. The desired result of church discipline is always repentance and the restoration of the offender. Our private and public disciplinary measures should always be undertaken in a spirit of love, gentleness, and humility as we seek to bring about this positive end (Galatians 6:1-2). When restoration does not occur and expulsion becomes necessary, we are glad to see the purity of Christ and the church upheld, but we should be grieved, individually and corporately, that someone we loved as an apparent brother or sister in Christ is now understood to be an unbeliever.

2. Genuine repentance consists of more than outward sorrow and tears (2 Corinthians 7:9-11). Repentance will be considered genuine when the offender not only leaves his sin, but also confesses it to all who are affected by it (even to the general membership of the church if necessary, as determined by the elders), and makes restitution when appropriate.

3. When a member is expelled or socially excluded, he or she may not attend any gathering of our church unless it is with the permission of the elders and for the purpose of public confession.* Members who have any necessary continuing association with an expelled person (e.g., husband/wife, parent/child, siblings, next-door neighbors, co-workers) must not participate with him or her in any shared activity that might be construed as Christian fellowship (1 Corinthians 5:11; 2 Corinthians 6:14-17; Ephesians 5:11). The manner of such association must also never imply approval of the offender's behavior and/or condemnation of the disciplinary action taken by the church (Proverbs 17:15).

4. In the case of a member who was expelled, restoration will be considered with great caution, and then only after the membership process is repeated in its entirety. Depending upon the nature of the offense, a restored member will not be immediately (if ever) qualified for biblical offices within the church (i.e., elder or deacon) due to a tarnished reputation, issues regarding marriage and divorce, and/or an obvious weakness in a particular area (1 Timothy 3:2-13; Titus 1:6-9; 1 Peter 5:3).

5. Disciplinary matters will be addressed promptly upon discovery of the sin. Unnecessary delay is harmful since it permits the perpetuation of the sin and causes an unhealthy tension within the church by creating the perception of apathy on the part of church leaders regarding sinful behavior.

---

*It is neither obedient to Christ, nor in the church's best interest, to permit an expelled person to attend the meetings of the church so that he can be exposed to biblical preaching. He was expelled because he has already heard, and *rejected*, the biblical message of repentance. The determination to exclude such a person from all church functions is primarily based on the command for Christians not to keep company with those who are under the discipline of expulsion (1 Corinthians 5:11), which in turn is based on the principle that "a little leaven leavens the whole lump" (1 Corinthians 5:6). Leaven (sinful influence) can only be prevented from spreading throughout the lump of dough (the church) when the two are not allowed to come into contact with each other. It cannot be right, therefore, to give a person who is openly unrepentant the opportunity to exert an immoral and/or divisive influence on the other members of a local church.

6. If an offending member leaves the church after initial disciplinary action begins, yet prior to expulsion from membership, the matter will still be brought to conclusion (meaning, formal expulsion will still occur as if the member were present). If it is discovered that a recently expelled member (or one who is fleeing disciplinary action) is seeking membership with another church (or has already become a member), one of our elders will, in most cases, attempt to arrange a private meeting with a pastor of that church (along with the offender, to avoid any appearance of slander), in order to disclose the offense and protect the other church from harm.

7. Paul's rebuke of the Corinthians in 1 Corinthians 6:1-8 is not a direct reference to a church discipline situation. However, the types of disputes among members that would necessitate a "church trial," as Paul describes, may often involve sinful behavior that should be dealt with through church discipline.

8. Every member of our church must agree that he or she will never initiate, pursue, or participate in any civil legal action against the church or against any member in connection with a disciplinary matter.* In fact, any Christian considering civil legal action against another Christian for any reason should consider Paul's prohibition of such behavior (1 Corinthians 6:1-8).

9. Persistent and willful non-attendance is a sin requiring church discipline (Hebrews 10:24-25). Except where persistent non-attendance is the result of unavoidable circumstances (e.g., extended illness or military service), it will be considered a public offense and addressed accordingly. Those who persist in their non-attendance without a legitimate excuse, even after exhortations and warnings from the church, will be expelled from membership.

---

*It is advisable for churches to include a statement regarding the issue of lawsuits in their membership agreement or church covenant. For an example of such a statement, see "The Fellowship of the Spirit" at www.ChristFellowshipKC.org.

No specific length of time has been established to designate non-attendance as "persistent." Each situation will be treated as unique. Without delay, our elders will be diligent in conducting the most thorough and comprehensive investigation possible in determining the reason(s) for non-attendance. Everyone should assume, until conclusive proof to the contrary exists, that the reason(s) are legitimate. Only when it becomes certain that the offender is willfully and sinfully avoiding our church meetings will he or she be disciplined.

10. A member who leaves our church is accountable to us, and remains under the supervision of our elders, until he joins another true church or is expelled. If the member lives locally and believes it is God's will for him to seek another church, the reasons must be discussed thoroughly with the elders. The member will remain under the counsel of the elders and the accountability of the church during this temporary process. If the member is unsuccessful in finding another church after a reasonable period of time, he must either return to regular attendance or be removed from our membership for non-attendance (see #9). The church will not retain non-attending members except due to illness, military service, or other extenuating circumstances.

If a member has moved out of town and we learn that he has not joined another true church within six months (unless a longer period of time is agreed upon with the elders), he will be removed from our membership. Certain exceptions apply, such as members who move to an area where there is no true church, or overseas military deployment. College and graduate students are expected to join a church near their school unless they are close enough to permit continued attendance with us.

If a member commits a disciplinable sin after moving out of town, the elders will do what is necessary to restore him and to help him find a local church where he can be cared for. If he will not repent, he will be removed immediately from our membership according to the normal process. Also, if a member leaves our church and joins a false church, cult, or non-Christian religion, he will be removed from our church.

11. Paul's words in 1 Timothy 5:19 ("Do not receive an accusation against an elder except from two or three witnesses.") should not be construed to mean that elders are to be protected from proper disciplinary action. Paul knew that elders, being in a position of authority, could easily become the objects of false or frivolous accusations. His command is simply a warning to watch for such abuses. Elders are church members just as all others, and are subject to discipline according to the same biblical principles as previously stated.

12. The training and discipline of children is the biblical obligation of parents, particularly fathers (Proverbs 13:24; 19:18; 23:13-14; Ephesians 6:4). Member-parents who refuse or neglect to properly train and discipline a child, resulting in the perpetuation of sinful behavior on the part of the child, are committing a public offense and are subject to church discipline. In the event that an older child has become a member, yet is living under parental authority, the parent(s) remain responsible. If the member-parent(s) of a member-child refuse or neglect to train and/or discipline, resulting in the perpetuation of the child's sinful behavior, both the member-parent(s) and the member-child are subject to the discipline of the church. This is not meant to refer to parents who *do* properly, diligently, and biblically train and discipline a particularly obstinate child who nevertheless remains rebellious and disobedient. Even in these rare cases, whether the child is a member or not, if his or her behavior is so disruptive, immoral, corrupting, divisive, and/or violent that the meetings of the church cannot proceed in a safe, peaceful, positive, pure, and orderly manner, he or she will be excluded from attendance or expelled from membership.

Final Thoughts

No church has a choice about obeying Christ, therefore our church must practice church discipline. But there is also beauty and value in disciplinary action that we may not immediately see. It is beautiful because it is about love. Our discipline toward a professing Christian in sin may be the most loving act he has ever experienced. However uninviting or difficult discipline might be, and however severely we must act, God has made church discipline valuable because it will either produce a holier life or a holier church, or both, when carried out obediently and harmoniously.

Key Passages of Scripture Regarding Church Discipline

Open rebuke is better than love carefully concealed.
~ *Proverbs 27:5*

Moreover if your brother sins against you, go and tell him his fault between you and him alone. If he hears you, you have gained your brother. But if he will not hear, take with you one or two more, that "by the mouth of two or three witnesses every word may be established." And if he refuses to hear them, tell it to the church. But if he refuses even to hear the church, let him be to you like a heathen and a tax collector.
~ *Matthew 18:15-17*

Now I urge you, brethren, note those who cause divisions and offenses, contrary to the doctrine which you learned, and avoid them.
~ *Romans 16:17*

It is actually reported that there is sexual immorality among you, and such sexual immorality as is not even named among the Gentiles—that a man has his father's wife. And you are puffed up, and have not rather mourned, that he who has done this deed might be taken away from among you. For I indeed, as absent in body but present in spirit, have already judged (as though I were present) him who has so done this deed. In the name of our Lord Jesus Christ, when you are gathered together, along with my spirit, with the power of our Lord Jesus Christ, deliver such a one to Satan for the destruction of the flesh, that his spirit may be saved in the day of the Lord Jesus. Your glorying is not good. Do you not know that a little leaven leavens the whole lump? Therefore purge out the old leaven, that you may be a new lump, since you truly are unleavened. For indeed Christ, our Passover, was sacrificed for us. Therefore let us keep the feast, not with old leaven, nor with the leaven of malice and wickedness, but with the unleavened bread of sincerity and truth. I wrote to you in my epistle not to keep company with sexually immoral people. Yet I certainly did not mean with the sexually immoral people of this world, or with the covetous, or extortioners, or idolaters, since then you would need to go out of the world. But now I have written to you not to keep company with anyone named a brother, who is sexually immoral, or coveteous, or an idolater, or a reviler, or a drunkard, or an extortioner—not even to eat with such a person. For what have I to do with judging those also who are outside? Do you not judge those who are inside? But those who are outside God judges. Therefore "put away from yourselves the evil person."

~ 1 Corinthians 5

Now I rejoice, not that you were made sorry, but that your sorrow led to repentance. For you were made sorry in a godly manner . . . For godly sorrow produces repentance leading to salvation, not to be regretted; but the sorrow of the world produces death. For observe this very thing, that you sorrowed in a godly manner: What diligence it produced in you, what clearing of yourselves, what indignation, what fear, what vehement desire, what zeal, what vindication! In all things you proved yourselves to be clear in this matter.

~ 2 Corinthians 7:9-11

Brethren, if a man is overtaken in any trespass, you who are spiritual restore such a one in a spirit of gentleness, considering yourself lest you also be tempted. Bear one another's burdens, and so fulfill the law of Christ.

~ Galatians 6:1-2

And have no fellowship with the unfruitful works of darkness, but rather expose them.

~ Ephesians 5:11

Now we exhort you, brethren, warn those who are unruly . . .

~ 1 Thessalonians 5:14

But we command you, brethren, in the name of our Lord Jesus Christ, that you withdraw from every brother who walks disorderly and not according to the tradition which he received from us. . . . And if anyone does not obey our word in this epistle, note that person and do not keep company with him, that he may be ashamed. Yet do not count him as an enemy, but admonish him as a brother.
~ *2 Thessalonians 3:6, 14-15*

This charge I commit to you, son Timothy, according to the prophecies previously made concerning you, that by them you may wage the good warfare, having faith and a good conscience, which some having rejected, concerning the faith have suffered shipwreck, of whom are Hymenaeus and Alexander, whom I delivered to Satan that they may learn not to blaspheme.
~ *1 Timothy 1:18-20*

Those who are sinning rebuke in the presence of all, that the rest also may fear.
~ *1 Timothy 5:20*

Reject a divisive man after the first and second admonition, knowing that such a person is warped and sinning, being self-condemned.
~ *Titus 3:10-11*

Pursue peace with all people, and holiness, without which no one will see the Lord: looking carefully lest anyone fall short of the grace of God; lest any root of bitterness springing up cause trouble, and by this many become defiled; lest there be any fornicator or profane person like Esau, who for one morsel of food sold his birthright.
~ *Hebrews 12:14-16*

Brethren, if anyone among you wanders from the truth, and someone turns him back, let him know that he who turns a sinner from the error of his way will save a soul from death and cover a multitude of sins.
~ *James 5:19-20*

Whoever transgresses and does not abide in the doctrine of Christ does not have God. . . . If anyone comes to you and does not bring this doctrine, do not receive him into your house nor greet him; for he who greets him shares in his evil deeds.
~ *2 John 9-11*